VOLUME 1 **BLOOD**

WONDER WOMAN

VOLUME 1: BLOOD

BRIAN **AZZARELLO** writer

CLIFF **CHIANG** artist

TONY **AKINS** artist (parts 5 & 6)

DAN **GREEN** additional inks (part 6)

MATTHEW **WILSON** colorist

JARED K. **FLETCHER** letterer

CLIFF **CHIANG** original series & collection cover artist

WONDER WOMAN created by WILLIAM MOULTON **MARSTON**

MATT IDELSON Editor – Original Series CHRIS CONROY Associate Editor – Original Series
PETER HAMBOUSSI Editor ROBBIN BROSTERMAN Design Director – Books
ROBBIE BIEDERMAN Publication Design

BOB HARRAS Senior VP – Editor-in-Chief, DC Comics

DIANE NELSON President DAN DIDIO and JIM LEE Co-Publishers
GEOFF JOHNS Chief Creative Officer
JOHN ROOD Executive VP – Sales, Marketing and Business Development
AMY GENKINS Senior VP – Business and Legal Affairs NAIRI GARDINER Senior VP – Finance
JEFF BOISON VP – Publishing Planning   MARK CHIARELLO VP – Art Direction and Design
JOHN CUNNINGHAM VP – Marketing TERRI CUNNINGHAM VP – Editorial Administration
ALISON GILL Senior VP – Manufacturing and Operations HANK KANALZ Senior VP – Vertigo and Integrated Publishing
JAY KOGAN VP – Business and Legal Affairs, Publishing JACK MAHAN VP – Business Affairs, Talent
NICK NAPOLITANO VP – Manufacturing Administration SUE POHJA VP – Book Sales
COURTNEY SIMMONS Senior VP – Publicity BOB WAYNE Senior VP – Sales

DC Comics, 1700 Broadway, New York, NY 10019
A Warner Bros. Entertainment Company
Printed by RR Donnelley, Salem, VA, USA. 7/5/13. Third Printing.
ISBN: 978-1-4012-3562-8

SUSTAINABLE   Certified Chain of Custody
FORESTRY   At Least 20% Certified Forest Content
INITIATIVE   www.sfiprogram.org
              SFI-01042
              APPLIES TO TEXT STOCK ONLY

Library of Congress Cataloging-in-Publication Data
Azzarello, Brian.
Wonder Woman volume 1 : blood / Brian Azzarello, Cliff Chiang, Tony Akins.
p. cm.
"Originally published in single magazine form in WONDER WOMAN
1-6"—T.p. verso.
ISBN 978-1-4012-3563-5
1. Graphic novels. I. Chiang, Cliff. II. Akins, Tony. III. Title.
PN6728.W6A97 2012
741.5'973—dc23
2011051798

SSSSHIIING

NO...

ZOLA, WE MUST LEAVE-- NOW.

WE? MAKE THAT *YOU*, MISTER. I DON'T KNOW HOW YOU GOT IN HERE--

--LISTEN TO ME, GIRL-- THEY'VE COME FOR YOU AND YOUR CHILD.

WHO?

ASSASSINS. IF WE DON'T--

--GET OUT OF MY HOUSE!

--YOU WILL *DIE* HERE!

HEY!

WHOOOSHHH

THUK

SLAM

HOLY...

WELL... THAT WAS STUPID.

YEAH? THERE'S NO WAY I WAS GONNA BE LEFT--

I MEANT OF ME.

YEEAARGH!

STAY CLOSE.

"AND A CAPE OF BLOOD, FLOWING FROM ITS SHOULDERS

"ONTO A NAKED WOMAN, AT ITS FEET."

"THE FEET?"

"THEY'RE BARE, LIKE THE WOMAN."

"THEN *IT* IS MY FAMILY."

"YOUR FAMILY...

"IS BROKEN

"BEATEN

"AND BETRAYED.

"BY BLOOD."

"TELL ME SOMETHING I DON'T KNOW..."

" WELL, YOUR FATHER HAS ABANDONED FATE

"TO SOMEONE WHO CAN BLOW AWAY THE SMOKE

"IF THEY CHOOSE TO. "SERIOUSLY, THIS IS MENTAL."

SSHKK

"WHAT DO YOU MEAN BY THAT?"

"WE MEAN THAT WHAT YOUR FATHER WANTS IS NOTHING ANYONE SHOULD."

"IT'S DIRTY, IT'S IRREDEEMABLE

"AND IT WON'T END GOOD FOR YOU."

I THOUGHT I TOLD YOU TO STAY CLOSE.

ZOLA... HER LIFE IS IMPORTANT.

THAT'S ONE THING MY LIFE *ISN'T!* MEANING *YOU'RE WRONG!*

YOU SAID THOSE THINGS WERE HERE TO KILL ME AND MY CHILD--WELL, I DON'T *HAVE* ONE!

GIRL...

YOU ARE PREGNANT.

SHE IS?

BY ZEUS.

OH, SH--

--EEEE!

--WILL KILL!

--ONE OF YOU.

ONE OF ME?

YEAH. ONE OF YOUR FATHER'S CHILDREN WILL MURDER ANOTHER AND TAKE THEIR PLACE.

IT'S WHAT YOUR FATHER WANTS.

THAT'S SO SCREWED UP.

THAT'S DEAR OLD DAD.

PULLING THE STRINGS, THE CURTAINS-- LEGS...

WHERE IS HE?

HE...

AS YOU SHOULDN'T. BUT ON THIS ISLAND, YOU MIGHT WANT TO KEEP THE **STORY** TO YOURSELF.

SPEAKING OF, WHAT'S WONDER WOMAN'S? SHE SEEMS DIFFERENT FROM THE REST.

INDEED SHE IS, GIRL.

"ACCORDING TO LEGEND, HIPPOLYTA--THE QUEEN-- HER WOMB WAS BARREN, YET SHE **DESPERATELY** WANTED A CHILD...

"SO ON A MOONLESS NIGHT, SHE FASHIONED A CHILD OUT OF CLAY...

"AND PRAYED TO THE GODS FOR A MIRACLE.

"WHEN SHE WAS DONE, SHE FELL EXHAUSTED...

"INTO DEEP SLUMBER...

"AND WITH THE SUN ABOVE, HIPPOLYTA WAS AWAKENED BY HER CHILD.

"WONDER WOMAN IS THE *PERFECT* AMAZON--NO MALE SEED CREATED HER."

THAT'S WEIRD.

MOST LEGENDS ARE.

"WHAT SAY YOU, DIANA..."

ON YOUR *KNEES*, INTRUDER, OR I SWEAR I'LL *PUT* YOU THERE!

WE ARE *SURROUNDED*, SISTERS! THESE WARRIORS ARE LIKE *NOTHING* WE'VE EVER FACED!

DIE, INVADER!

PARADISE ISLAND.

ALEKA, LOOK AT WHAT WE'VE LOST...

I'M ASHAMED.

YOU'RE WHAT? WHY? DID YOU BRING THE MUSK--

--DIVINE AS IT MAY BE-- TO OUR ISLAND? OR THE MORTAL?

IT WASN'T YOU, DAPHNE...

IT WAS CLAY.

CLAY?

ALEKA... NO!

YES. I HAVE NO REASON TO HOLD MY TONGUE WHEN WHAT I TRULY HOLD DEAR IS THREATENED.

WE ARE ABOUT TO BURN OUR OWN... BUT *I* BURN AS WELL!

AMAZONS, WE HAVE BEEN *COMPROMISED.*

PARADISE IS *RUINED.*

OUR PASSION LEFT ME PREGNANT, AND TO GUARD THAT SECRET, I LEFT HIM. HE DID NOT FOLLOW.

QUICKLY I LEARNED, POSSESSING A GOD HAS SCANT TO DO WITH KEEPING HIM.

I WASN'T MADE OF CLAY.

I HAD TO PROTECT YOU FROM HERA! SHE'S--

EVERYTHING I SAID SHE WAS. IF SHE KNEW--

DIANA, YOU'D BE DEAD.

OR WORSE.

IF MY LIFE IS A LIE, CAN IT BE WORSE THAN DEATH?

ABSOLUTELY.

WE HATCHED A PLAN, PRINCESS, AND IT KEPT YOU SAFE.

WE? THIS WAS A CONSPIRACY? MOTHER? WHY...?

DON'T CALL
ME THAT--
OR CLAY--
EVER AGAIN...

DIANA...

"...OUT OF OUR CONTROL."

LONDON.

AND DON'T GET YOUR FEATHERS--OR SHOULD I SAY FEATHER--RUFFLED.

I MEAN, THERE'S SOMETHING TO BE SAID FOR LEVITY AT A TIME LIKE THIS.

THEN LET'S NOT KID AROUND. HERA WILL HAVE HER POUND OF FLESH...

INDEED. SO PERHAPS IF WE EXTRACTED IT FOR HER...

CHUKK

QUEEN HIPPOLYTA...

NEVER MIND, WHAT I WAS SAYING IS THAT IT'S ONLY MY HOME BECAUSE I *NEVER* LEFT IT.

MY HOUSE IS THERE. NOTHING ELSE.

I LEFT *MY* HOME...THE FACT THAT I WAS CREATED FROM CLAY, IT MADE ME...I DIDN'T BELONG. I FELT DIFFERENT FROM ALL MY SISTERS.

BUT THAT'S NOT A FACT ANYMORE.

AND I CAN'T TALK ABOUT SISTERS, 'CAUSE I WASN'T LUCKY ENOUGH TO HAVE ANY FAMILY OF ANY KIND.

LIKE MY FATHER? HE'S IN PRISON, HAS BEEN SINCE I WAS A BABY.

WHAT DID HE DO?

SOMETHING REALLY BAD. THAT'S WHAT GETS YOU LOCKED UP FOR LIFE.

AND MY MOTHER?

SHE MADE MISTAKES TOO. AND LORD KNOWS I NEVER LET HER OFF THE HOOK...

THEN SHE *DIED*.

SO *MY* HOME? IT'S JUST A WORD.

I'M PROBABLY BETTER OFF WITHOUT IT, HUH?

HE LOVES US?

HEH. I SAID *SURPRISING*, NOT *SHOCKING*...

HE'S GONE MISSING. ACTUALLY, ACCORDING TO MY ORACLES, HE DOESN'T EXIST.

"MURDERED?"

"IT WOULD TAKE HIS *OWN* BLOOD TO DO SO."

"AH. NOW I UNDERSTAND THE PLEASURE OF THIS VISIT."

SORRY TO DISAPPOINT YOU, APOLLO, BUT NONE OF THIS BLOOD BELONGS TO ZEUS.

FRANKLY, I COULDN'T BE BOTHERED.

THAT'S NOT WHY I'M HERE. BUT--

GIVEN YOUR DISPOSITION--IT'S NOT OUT OF THE QUESTION THAT OTHERS IN OUR FAMILY MIGHT THINK THAT. YOU COULD USE AN *ALLY*.

ME?

OR YOU?

GIVEN YOUR *SUNNY* DISPOSITION, I IMAGINE THIS IS AN *OPPORTUNITY*, EH?

WELL, THE GLASS IS HALF FULL...

YOU WANT TO BE KING?

HAVE AT IT.

I'LL SIT THIS ONE OUT.

NO, HERMES. GIVEN THE SHAPE YOU'RE IN, AND ZOLA'S CONDITION--

WHAT?

I'M NOT EVEN *SHOWING* YET!

--IF I CONFRONT HERA, IT LEAVES YOU TWO--

MONSTER PULLED FROM THAMES

--*THREE.*

--UNPROTECTED. I CAN'T ALLOW THAT.

ONE WAY OF LOOKING AT IT.

YOU HAVE ANOTHER?

'ERE YOU GO, MISS.

HERA KNOWS YOU'RE ZEUS' DAUGHTER. KEEPING ZOLA CLOSE MAY ACTUALLY MAKE HER MORE VULNERABLE.

TOMATOES FOR BREAKFAST?

IT'S PROPER.

NOT WHERE I'M FROM.

NOR I.

COLOR'S A BIT OFF, IN'NIT? NOT SANGUINE ENOUGH FOR YOU, MESSENGER?

I IMAGINE YER USED TO WINE, BREAKFAST, LUNCH, AN' SUPPER...

IT EXPLAINS YER KIND'S MOODS.

BRING US A PINT, LUV.

MIND IF I SIT?

WHO ARE YOU?

ME? A MAN WITH THE ADVANTAGE...

SEE, I KNOW WHO YOU ARE.

WELL, TWO A' YOU, ANYWAY.

WE WERE HAVING A PRIVATE CONVERSATION.

PRIVATE? 'FRAID THAT'S BEEN BLOWN OFF THE TABLE.

THE WIND, NOISE TO MOST, SURE. 'CAUSE EVERY WORD THAT'S SPOKEN, SHE CARRIES.

BUT WORDS CAN BE SUSSED OUT, IF ONE CARES TO GIVE A LISTEN...

I DON' THINK SO. WITH YOU, SOME JUS' DON' GET THE MESSAGE, EH?

YOU'RE CLEVER.

IS NICE TO HEAR.

BE THAT AS IT MAY, THE WIND TELLS ME...

NOW THAT ZEUS IS GONE, HIS BROTHERS MAY BE LOOKING TO CARVE UP WHAT HE'S LEFT BEHIND.

AN' THE GODS, THEY CAN BE DOWNRIGHT EVIL ABOUT THINGS, EH, MESSENGER?

DIANA, IF WHAT LENNOX SAYS IS TRUE--

I'VE DEALT WITH EVIL BEFORE.

AM I DEALING WITH IT NOW?

WELL, YOU'LL EXCUSE ME BEIN' CAGEY, BUT THAT'S WHAT I'M HERE TO FIND OUT.

LET ME LEVEL. I'VE MIXED IT UP WITH BAD MEN IN MY TIME...

BUT THEY WAS JUST MEN. TODAY, I'M GETTIN' INTA SOMETHIN' I'VE AVOIDED FOR MORE THAN EIGHTY YEARS.

EIGHTY-- BUT YOU DON'T LOOK--

--OR YOU DON'T SEE THE FAMILY RESEMBLANCE...

...LITTLE *SISTER!?* I CAN'T BELIEVE YOU FELL FOR THAT CREEP'S LINE.

UNDERSTOOD, ZOLA. BUT WHAT IF HE *IS* FAMILY?

FROM WHAT I'VE SEEN? YOU CAN DO WITHOUT YOUR NEW FAMILY.

HMM. I HAVE TO *LIVE* WITHOUT MY OLD ONE.

OH, JEEZ... I'M--

--PART OF MY NEW FAMILY...

I MEAN, YOU'RE MY... AUNT?

NOT 'TIL THE BABY'S BORN!

IT'S SO WEIRD. YOU BEING OLDER THAN ME, AND I'M GONNA GIVE BIRTH-- TO YOUR...

I THINK IT'S A BOY.

MY BROTHER, THEN. AND IT'S NO WEIRDER THAN WHAT LENNOX CLAIMS.

I BELIEVE WHAT HE SAID MAY BE TRUE. THAT HE LEARNED WHO HE WAS... WHAT DID HE CALL IT?...

"...GOING TO WAR FOR THEM WITH THE FATE OF THE WORLD HANGING IN THE BALANCE.

"GOOD AGAINST EVIL...

"WINNER TAKE ALL.

"THAT IS SOMETHING I BELIEVE IN.

"OR *WANT* TO..."

IT'S KINDA COOL.

UM, WONDER WOMAN, I THINK YOU'RE MISSING SOME OF THE OTHER THINGS LENNOX SAID.

LIKE WHAT?

MY NAME IS DIANA.

MY MOTHER IS...

WAS-- HIPPOLYTA.

I REQUEST AN AUDIENCE...

"...MONGREL.

"MY BROTHER ZEUS WAS A MONSTER WHO CARED ABOUT NOTHING OTHER THAN *HIMSELF.*

"ERGO, I'M NOT INTERESTED IN ANYTHING YOU HAVE TO SAY.

"AND NOW THAT THE HEAVENS ARE WITHOUT A LORD...

"I MEAN TO CLAIM THEM AS *MINE*...

...BUT I AM AFRAID *HERA* CLAIMS THE HEAVENS AS *HERS.*

WHAT?!

SHE *DARES?!?*

"THIS WORLD WAS DIVIDED AMONG THREE BROTHERS. THE HEAVENS, THE SEAS, AND THE UNDERWORLD.

"THE *SCRAPS* WE LEFT TO OTHERS.

"I CAN UNDERSTAND HOW THE SCRAPS MAY BE LACKING, BECAUSE THE *SEAS* CERTAINLY ARE. BUT...

"THE SEAS NOW HOLD THE *POWER.*

"I CAN DESTROY THE SCRAPS, OR THE *OTHERS* CAN BE HAPPY WITH THEM.

"IT'S THEIR CHOICE TO OPPOSE ME."

WHAT IF THE QUEEN SEES THINGS DIFFERENTLY?

WITHOUT A KING, THE QUEEN HAS *NOTHING!*

NOTHING... AS IN NOTHING TO LOSE. I WOULD THINK YOU MIGHT FIND A WOMAN IN THAT POSITION--

--FORMIDABLE.

YES. I FIND A WOMAN IN ANY POSITION TO BE SUCH.

SPOKEN LIKE A MAN WHO UNDERSTANDS THEM.

REALLY?

AND HERE I WAS SAYING THAT THEY'RE NOTHING BUT A MYSTERY.

TAKES A SMART MAN TO ADMIT WHAT 'E DON' KNOW. AN ADMIRABLE TRAIT.

CRACK

THWACK

ZOLA,
DIDN'T
I TELL
YOU...

...TO STAY CLOSE?

SCREW YOU! THIS IS *NO* POSITION FOR A WOMAN IN MY CONDITION TO *BE* IN!

NO, IT ISN'T...

SO THIS AIN'T GOING ACCORDING TO LENNOX'S PLAN...

NOT ON THIS END, YET. LET'S HOPE LENNOX IS FARING BETTER...

I FIND THIS FASCINATING.

WHA' *THIS?*

THIS PLAYING WITH GODS. IT NEVER ENDS WELL FOR YOU, BECAUSE IT ACTUALLY IS *ONLY* A GAME TO US. YET YOU INSIST...

IS THAT HERMES?

IS. I'M RUNNIN' WITH THE MESSENGER.

HEH.

HA HA

I MAKE A JOKE?

NO. YES-- I'M SORRY...

YOU SAID YOU'RE RUNNING WITH SOMEONE YOU CAN'T *POSSIBLY* KEEP UP WITH.

WELL, WAS JUS' A TURN OF PHRASE.

HEH. PERHAPS *YOUR* WORDS WERE.

'E'S A BIT LARGER THAN I IMAGINED.

YOU'RE STILL A PUPPY. YOU'LL FIND, IN TIME, THAT IMAGINATION IS JUST WHAT OTHERS USE TO GET THINGS THEY CAN'T UNDERSTAND INTO THEIR HEADS...

RARELY--IF EVER--DO THEY ACTUALLY FIT THERE.

NOW, SEA...

WHAT DO YOU THINK OF HEAVEN'S BASTARDS' PROPOSAL?

THEIR WHAT?

YOU NEVER LET ME FINISH.

BECAUSE I AM FINISHED WITH YOU. I DON'T-- I CAME HERE FOR ONE THING--

--AS DID I. BUT WHAT THEY PROPOSE...IT'S DELICIOUS.

WHICH IS?

WHAT IF HEAVEN WERE RULED BY DAY BY THE SEA... AND BY NIGHT BY SHADOW--

SHARING A QUEEN?

HAA

BWAA-HAA

SO HERA RETAINS HER POSITION, BUT UNDER TWO KINGS?

THAT *IS* PRICELESS...

HEH HEH

ISN'T IT?

MIND IF I 'AVE ME LIGHT, NOW?

OF COURSE. THIS IS--

BOOOOM

--NOT COMING TO PASS!

YOUR LAUGHTER IS LIKE THE SQUEALING OF PIGS...

DISRESPECTFUL TO BOTH ME AND YOUR BROTHER.

WHY, IF ZEUS WERE HERE TO HEAR, HE WOULD *BREAK* YOUR BONES.

HE'S NOT, THOUGH, IS HE?

NO, HE ISN'T. GONE INTO THE ETHER, IT SEEMS. HEAVEN HAS LEFT HIS THRONE WANTING AN ASS TO *WARM* IT.

AND THOUGH BOTH OF YOU CERTAINLY QUALIFY IN THAT REGARD, NEITHER OF YOU MEASURE UP...

TO MINE.

REALLY? YOURS IS QUITE FRIGID, NO?

THIS IS NOT A GAME!

THE LADY, SHE'S RIGHT.

SNAP

?

WHAT DO YOU THINK YOU'RE **DOING,** MESSENGER?

SENDING A MESSAGE.

"TO WHOM?"

"TO YOU, HERA."

?

NO...

YES.

NOOOO--

BOOOM

SSSSS

--OOoo!

YOU *ARROGANT*-- COMING TO *MY* HOUSE...

I WILL *DESTROY* YOU--

YOUR ACTIONS ALREADY HAVE, GODDESS. AND I WILL SPEND MY DAYS...

MAKING YOU *REGRET* THEM.

YOU...YOU'RE MADE OF STONE?

SOMETHIN' LIKE THAT. IS ME DEE EN AYE...

DOES IT HURT?

JUS' TO LOOK AT.

BWAA...

HAA HAA HAA.

SEEMS WE'VE BEEN PLAYED FOR FOOLS, BROTHER.

YES. AND DESERVEDLY.

OH, LIGHTEN UP.

I'M AFRAID I CAN'T.

SO THIS WAS ALL ABOUT BLINDING HERA FOR YOU?

NO. PROTECTING A MOTHER AND HER CHILD.

"AH, SO YOU HAVE CONCEIT, MY AMAZON NIECE..."

...YOU'LL FIT RIGHT IN.

ALL IN ALL, I'D SAY--

--WE GOT LUCKY.

HERA TOOK THE BAIT, POSEIDON WAS AMUSED, AND HADES STORMED OFF.

SOMETIMES, LUCK IS ENOUGH, EH...

...ZOLA?

MOM?

BABY...

ZOLA--!! DON'T--

SHLOCK

ZOLA!

DIANA!

DIANAAAA!

WE STRUCK A *BARGAIN*, WONDER WOMAN.

FULFILL YOUR END, OR ZEUS' BLOODLINE...

"ENDS WITH YOU."

HERMES

CLIFF
CHANG
2011

HERMES IV
CLIFF
CHIANG
2011

HERMES V a
CLIFF
CHIANG
2011

ZOLA II
CLIFF
CHANG
2011

Apollo

CLIFF
CHIANG
2011

ARES

STRIFE
CLIFF
CHIANG
2011

HERA
CLIFF
CHIANG
2011

Designs for Hippolyta, the Amazons and the male and female centaurs.